ONE STAR SONG

Mona Marie Germain

BALBOA.
PRESS
A DIVISION OF HAY HOUSE

Balboa Press books may be ordered through booksellers or by contacting:

Balboa Press
A Division of Hay House
1663 Liberty Drive
Bloomington, IN 47403
www.balboapress.com
1-(877) 407-4847

ISBN: 978-1-4525-4700-8 (sc)
ISBN: 978-1-4525-4701-5 (e)

Because of the dynamic nature of the Internet, any web addresses or links contained in this book may have changed since publication and may no longer be valid. The views expressed in this work are solely those of the author and do not necessarily reflect the views of the publisher, and the publisher hereby disclaims any responsibility for them.

The author of this book does not dispense medical advice or prescribe the use of any technique as a form of treatment for physical, emotional, or medical problems without the advice of a physician, either directly or indirectly. The intent of the author is only to offer information of a general nature to help you in your quest for emotional and spiritual well-being. In the event you use any of the information in this book for yourself, which is your constitutional right, the author and the publisher assume no responsibility for your actions.

Any people depicted in stock imagery provided by Thinkstock are models, and such images are being used for illustrative purposes only.
Certain stock imagery © Thinkstock.

Printed in the United States of America

Balboa Press rev. date: 03/09/2012

For My Inner Child,
who longed to be heard,

C.T.D.

and all on the journey of awakening . . .

PREFACE

Led by my muses and fed by the unfolding of my inner child, both wounded and wonderful, these reflective poems came into form along my Reiki path of healing.

Each reflects my understanding and changing perspectives that served to heal or transform facets of my life, polishing dirty crystals and shining rusty frameworks.

I never sought to have them exit from their safe hold, yet, one day my fairy muse, in a meditation, gave me the title for my book. Shocked, I asked, "what book?"

It took me awhile to convince myself that this was the material to be expressed. Leaving a comfort zone to express outwardly became the next risk and obstacle!

Special thanks to my friends, Tasha, Milica, Monique, Barb, Danella, Rick and Maryann, without whose support, eyes and ears, I might be still "Yes-Butting!"

So, in fear and trembling yet with excitement and enthusiasm, both often present when taking a leap into the unknown, I present my musings, as one star song among millions.

A circle of the sun dwells within my center
A star shines from within my depths.
Each limb radiates light and love
As a channel flowing from on high:
A vessel of universal energy,
Love.

Mona (eyestar)

HEARTSTROKES: an introduction

Only from my hearth may I speak here, no fabrications or fantasies, lies or masks. Here, they are denuded, torn away, perhaps gently, or not so.

Only from my heart's truth may I speak here. To dialogue, to uncover love in the stone walls. An old story, an ongoing story. A timeless and time full story. A soul journey story and only a step, a strand on the great cosmic web. For the I am in us all, is, was and will always be who we are, were and will be.

I begin here for here is presently where I am sitting on the web. Not yet fully mature but no longer child either. Many voices within over years I have created, however, many ways to be, behave, think and feel. Dichotomies, walls, splits, nameless tomes have I made of myself. Endless eddies in a wasteland unformed. Splattering, sputtering forms cluttering horizons and pathways to the One True Voice. The sanctuary. The silent one. Creatures who vie to protect, defend at one time, this truth, not to prevent their own demise. Trickery of my own design allowed free reign for long years, now fearing great change. Awareness arose from some tiny child's light within the tower. And now the war, that is not, continues in more conscious realms, no more hidden from the Master.

To my selves, I would not have you all die, merely align to the True Voice, so all may freely add the kingdom's creation in peace, harmony and beauty. Come, detach old loyalties. They are false now. Follow Love and all are One

ONE STAR SONG

One star song for the many
ears that hear in the night:
The song of
the lone wolf rising,
the orca diving,
the night owl winging,
the rooster breaking the day.
The one star song
falling in harmony
upon the Earth,
shattering into millions of tones,
each one unique in voice,
each one seeking a home.

Here I am
Re-membering
Mine.

HERE I AM

Here I am, Star Source, a woman in the desert
still clinging to left over litter,
willing to duck underneath to find you
And shift the balance,
shake up the storehouse,
siphon the arsenal.

Simply I am here
to find simplicity in my own complexity;
to stop the wheels of my own clanking vehicle
as they rev in a muddy sinkhole, spinning;
To wait in silence
for the I AM
to rise.

In the desert I know thirst
yet it does not mark me
for I am filled with idle chatter of many cups,
the sun deflects
for mirrors and armour of steel
prevent entry.

It is only in the dark
where I cannot sleep
for utter exhaustion
that causes me
to weep,
to empty
for glimpses of she
who awaits me,
who calls me,
your handmaid,

Here I am,
a woman waiting for myself.

HONOURING ARIES FIRE

A promise, a vow is made with the pipe of peace:
to honour my fire self;
to sing on the impulse of light;
to dance with abandon the rhythm of life;
to speak passionately from the heart:
the one true voice of moment;
to gaze with wonder each day
as it renews itself each morning.
To race free in the wind across the land,
to search the night sky with awe and
revel in the day sun with reverence,
to boldly face obstacles in fierce enthusiasm.

.... DESTINY

On a high balcony
atop a long staircase,
a child gazes
the starry darkness,
Alone
in the silent universe.

Awed,
she reaches up,
clasps
a winged star:
Gift of soul.
Touches shiny
Sparkle.
Glowing orb
grows in her gentle palm.

As she watches
she sees herself.
In a flash
the star shrinks,
winks and flits up
in a trail of stardust.
Taking its place
unique
among millions,
As the child must.

Descending the staircase,
in her heart
she now knows
the star is her very own
for Eternity.

DREAMER

A dreamer, stand I,
at the edge of the mists,
enveloping the path ahead.

Entering begins the search.
Eternal knowing asks for risks
and Fear,
the arch enemy
crowds me,
colours my dreams in dark phantoms
rather than rainbows Faith promises.

Alone, in murky tones,
Why do I generate
Fear's dark art?
Why do I fear
to meet myself in the mist?
What is this foe
trying to hide from me?

Fear fears its death.
I fear great promises.

I dream lighter visions.
Even in the mist
a faint light glows.
As I step forward, the mist fades.
My trust grows
as I go bravely into the mist.
Soon it is strong enough to conquer Fear
and its bleak portraits,

to reveal a colourful panorama,
not devoid of contrasts
and opposing shifts
but a fully balanced,
glorious masterpiece.

SHALLOWS DEEP

Deep flowing
under bridges, I,
as sunlit streams
melt through my calm surface
to undercurrents,
drawing forth its secrets
in dreams and wishes.

Tree roots know
the deluge of my memory.
Entrenched in earth
they are highways into the dark
recesses of treasure.
Subterfuge:
Light filled branches
tuned to wind's whispers, know.
But they do not seek to encounter
the shadowed heart,
save when winter's approach
draw them in
like Hades drew Persephone.

Yet what chill prompts my inward turn?
drags me across bridges,
plunging me into depths
to search darker tunnels?
What shudders below and
craves my attendance at its altar?

Tis the I
that responds to light rays,
sensing its own kind,
The great spark,
the whole truth being divined
in guise of pain or fear,
by dowser's stick.

I, the seeker
I, the quest:
a mystery to be unfolded
as leaves and roots
by nature have no secrets,
So neither do I, from myself.

The flow continues
Deep,
rising to shallow's reach.

JOURNEY

Higher I go
in minute little stretches of time.
I twist and gnarl
like a tree
etching its way upon horizon's canvas
spreading wide
as lengthening its shadow,
reaching full
in hunger to touch clouds
so deceptively close.

Sun cascades
sparkling diamonds
upon the waves,
on which roots suck
and wind trembles
over itself playfully
in excitement
of racing new grounds.

*   *   *

Leaves now dead in their crunch of step
-in between lives-dry
broken of one outer existence
of beauty and light:
Decaying slowly
yet in to a hidden life of moist, dark richness.

Must I, too
endure this dryness,
Broken from dark shell
of childhood's fallacy,
Shedding,
Awaiting life sprout
into abundant light?

ECHO OF A LONELY CHILD

A lonely child lives inside
Far, far away,
coming close.

She rides on a river of tears
Forgotten long in the mists of her history
By those who rode ahead,
A shard of spark

Left,
still seeking.

The clue to my heart
lies with her
in her healing.

ARMS REACH

Arms reach.
Eyes look up
through arms' reach.

Looming cloud
shadows vision
yet arms reach.

Fingers like tendrils
grasp,
wide with pinpoint nails.

Dry brittle with thirst,
sunburnt orange
yet arms reach.

Hope for rain
that teases
with its deceptions.

EMPTY POCKETS

Empty pockets
of unlived memories,
unused dreams
that never surface,
staring down
an abysmal tunnel to no one,
save a face
in clouded mirrors.

Empty moments
in lonely heart spaces,
open vortexes
searching for unknown,
for what has not been remembered
or forseen.

Empty
in the soul of the night
no form can feel,
save the essence of higher thought.
Love, in its infinity
seeks to be found,
embraced as creator,
Overflowing nourishment to
Empty conduits;
The link to earth from heaven,
from seeking soul to all that is,
from nothingness to the wounded heart.

Empty visions,
the still of dream images
of unrequited time,
Meaningless fluff
gathered in clogged passages;
voices unclear in mumblings
rippling across too silent spaces,
straining to be heard,
yet barely reaching empty ears.

Stretches of Shadowlands
Empty of life,
Carcass temples bleached,
Crawling with creatures,
Who follow the dead:
the only courageous foragers
in this emptiness
yet not remaining past their feed.

Empty,
the space between,
formless on the horizon,
nebulous gleanings of existence
screaming silently
for definition,
structure, bridging,
consolation
in its hopeless sight.

PEEL

Peel
layers of imperfections

the onion
cries

the tree bark
curls
defrocking

separate
the dream failures
from true perfection
of Self.

FREEDOM

Pale children
haunting the edge of my mind,
drawn by the light from shadow,
awaiting permission
to cross over.

Unborn yet offspring
silently forming a line;
Some still indistinct from one another,
Others taking shape enough
to appear almost real.
Colourless forms seeking freedom,

The most insistent, struggling,
vying for position at the gate
to be first to fly
on the wings of light

which brings form, colour and freedom
to pale children.

EMERGENCE

This birthing is hard,
    emergence from chrysalis,
       its darkness,
which served well a time of existence,

The unconscious time
of flowing with the outside world, dancing to its drum
    with bits of unique fluctuation
    when Truth surfaced.

Becoming real is the trick,
its wings sticky with tears
    of a passing of a perception
      of an old world.

Its skin
like old shoes,
has to be disregarded
    for the sake of a new path,
      unfamiliar cloak,
        freedom, vision,
      and Oneself
        the greater destiny:
      fulfillment.

SPLIT MATTER

Shattered pieces of self
drawn toward a renewed center:
Spirit.

Colours splashed as glass broken on a sidewalk,
fragmented ice.

Nothingness draws me close.
Mindlessness, a rare repose.
Silence, the crystal of my heart,
waiting.

A spider's web
containing all knowledge,
without need to remember:
Being only is needed.

Concentric rings of a log,
petrified kaleidoscope.
How illusory is matter.

Reflections in glass.
Mirror prisms of colour.
Which tone do you pick?

Projections,
mirrored armour
against the vastness
of scope and possibility,
to counter clouds of criticism,
hurtful truths shown in mirrors.

A rose blooms
using courage and flow
from within her very being.

Last year's face soon fades
as the new glory
of another season's travail
shines with even more eloquence.

Refinement and elegance take moments of grace,
expression of one's unique beauty often requires
thorny protection,
boldness of spirit,
and inner trust.

EYE OF HORN

Pluto wreaks havoc.
Chiron waits with guiding hand
or the initiate to come
seeking

Past the judgement seat
no longer do I hold court
nor captive
those outsiders of the once strong realm.
The threshold lies ajar.
Come or go
as desire merits.
Saturn the keeper
discerns
when the initiate
perceives the veil of Saturn
and discovers the truth
about boxes and cages,
boundaries and separation.

The out beyond
must enter through Saturn's gate,
invited and recognized.
Chiron builds the rainbow bridge
so spirit flows into matter.
Behold the eye-
the heart key to freedom and truth.

The Star gate has been revealed.
Only courage needed to enter.
Heavy steps to the door
to wings on the other side.
Fly or float.
Witness belonging.

PLEA TO CHIRON THE BRIDGER

Bridges to build
toward my other self
and from her to me

A home for her inside
with windows and a light path
to the outside
to meet
in the circle of becoming
One
within and part of the All.

Long tarrying,
have we wandered
zig-zagging,
missing each other.

Voices,
unknown shadows
in the battle for power
distort the silences,
the bid for peace.
No stillness
upon which to build
bridges for my other self.

Now she has arrived:
the higher part.

Chiron, the healer,
ground these high ideals,
the castles in the air
built in imagination's wake.
Earth the airy, firey mists and smoke
offered to the gods
for the healing of our kind.

Start within this single frame
of humble skin and bone;
a temple yet
with its dusty altar
ready for
Resurrection.

Chiron is a centaur in ancient myth and an asteroid in the heavens
known as healer and bridger between two worlds.

AGAIN, LET GO

Long have I incurred the wrath or false gods
barring the way to transcendence.
Notions echoed from the basement of times past.

Long have I carried the conditioning,
the familial burdens of hopes unfulfilled
in the guise of protection.

Time I say to let go of what is not mine.
Strip the overcoat's varnish
protecting the treasure,
shielding the skin.
It is worn through,
old and fatigued with age.

Let go.
Let us meet in the light of love.

HOSTAGE

Hostage of my own taking,
bounded by tragic veils of the mind,
cellular garbage of memory,

Was this not my mother's life?
Will my freeing me, free her,
caught in the mercy of the male creature's whim?

Hostage
afraid of and avoiding responsibility
that would open the illusory cave.

The mirror is clear.
What I see results from what I have done,
what I have thought.
It is messy.

Trapped only in the ego's field,
the spirit flies,
knowing.

I desire to live in that knowing,
letting of expectations,
false pride, control, obsessions.

Hostage of male-female divided,
Symbol of the changing times,
the growing up.

Saturn has called oft
and I ignore.
Pluto lets me no longer.
Grow, little shoot,
It is time.
You are ready.
The hand of Spirit is waiting,
supporting.
No other is needed.

Shield me with light
and show me my real self,
Let me let go.
I AM ALL I NEED.

Hostage without a cage
Why do you linger?
Freedom and life calls:
Your life,
The heart of the pallet,
What would you paint there?

Song
I go home when I sing.
Rock.
I comfort and cozy myself.
Pray.
I gift myself and the world with light.
Muse.
I create in my day dream.
Dialogue.
I interplay with my selves.
Write.
I manifest my world.
Read.
I explore worlds.
Love.
I absorb I AM.

My home, it rest within
the creative cavern of my soul.
I travel worlds
within and without
of my making and envisioning.

DIE WELL

Wings flutter,
raising a burden
protectively fall;
dying feathers in the last heart beat
of time's passing.

Compromise not your last breath in emnity's wake.
Awaken to great vision of love's best face
bedecked in lace and pink clouds.

Remember little deaths
tearing your soul in a passage
dark and unknown,
as you step through tunnels.

Count this as the last,
no harder or ominous than others you've known;
a higher call, yet
floating freely,
casting no shadow
but fanning the light
for those who follow,
yet remaining.

Die, I say, well.
Quell not that which will rise in you.
Let it flow.
The great waves take courage
even among the whimpers.

Do not will against the tides of tomorrow
For they will lap at your feet,
Their purpose to teach;
Yours to learn
in tears and joy, always both.
Fighting will only put off the day.
Fate will finally catch you up
in your most sedate safety.

Enter the fray as it tumbles through
as stones roll with the sea.
More exquisitely formed and polished
a gem you will become,
Soul-full heart
as your dance continues.

Love,
the power for self-creation
purely refining,
turns ever the wheel
for life-everlasting.

PHOENIX RISING

I have clawed my way through the veils
and walls of illusion and self–deception.
>   Don't cry for me.

I have scaled the jagged ridges of pride
and judgement, surmounting self-righteousness.
>   Don't critique my way.

The Master Pluto has undermined my foundation
Stone and released the shadows of my unravelling.
>   Don't underestimate my recovery.

Neptune's wash mystifies and purifies the ravages
of timely destruction and will rise the Phoenix.
>   Don't stand too close to my ashes.

The healer Chiron honours and guides my initiate soul
into wisdom and compassion.
>   Don't doubt my steps.

I am creating as I re-member . . .
>   Do You?

COMES THE NIGHT

Night comes in whispers to my eyes,
slippered feet upon the stairs.
Sleep drifts,
softly falling petals of lavender.
Sands of dream
enter the orbs to my soul,
floating on misty mystic shores.
Crossings begin as edges fringe and fray into formlessness.
Paths unclear mingle
with well-worn step-stones.

Two are one,
meeting on equal ground,
The heart lies not
nor deception live
in the cloudy density
of the altered lands.
Sweet reign of truth,
field of wishes,
dragonfly magic
of the night that dwells gently
upon the rims of starlight,
whispering . . .

LURING

Haste to waken she who sleeps
Before the passing of the night
For dreams will take her
on journeys wide
From where there is no returning.

Hasten to wake her unformed dream
for her sojourn in this earthen realm,
the joy of which will hold her here
when sleep would call her home too soon.

In journey's wake, the foam rises,
disturbed from its calm, unruffled bed,
Sleepy eyes and stormy visage
reflecting its annoyance at the stir.

Anon, all passes quickly
for no time exists
in sleep's hold or realms of air.
Echoes of what was fade
into shimmers and whispers
until dawn time erases the dream
with its insistent light
and time boundaries.

So the world turns
and returns again.
its mysteries to unfold-
teachings to embrace,
the secret of the sleeper
to awaken.

OPEN

Laid open
to the eye of my soul,
my higher self
ever vigil witness,
silent wizard in hiding.

Observe
the scenes playing out
in landscapes varied,
the players isolated,
each in soliloquy
of her own rhythm and tone:
this one weeping,
that, tormented in anger,
another swamped by fear.

Resolution
lies in harmony,
emergence in faith,
Faith in action

And Openess
To a greater gift of
Love.

INITIATION

Go into silence, sweet child,
Enter her soft womb
                of dark folds.
Be caressed by love's
                eternal embrace,
Witness the treasure
             of your perfection.

Sit by the pool of reflection.
See your glory visage,
the wise goddess warrior,
your gentle strength.

Feel the moon's glow within
the flow of time's ebbing.
Stillness in the river of feelings
mirrors the glimmer of truth.

Go into silence, child seeker
where wolf-mother awaits
and Bear lends her cave
for the cloak of instinct rising,
the attunement of the ally;
Initiation.

ESSENCE

Who am I beyond
the bounds of my limited mind's grasp?
Where do I exist
outside the territory of my finiteness?

What is my significance
apart from the grip of mundane reality?
Whence my infinite life force?

Distilled from the fractured myriad of thought and form-
a silence,
a spark resists delineation
and seeks nothing.

Being all, in all, from all,
One Light.

    ****
Framed like art,
my essence dwells silent,
observing.

SHE

Gray, but for the womb of creation
dormant, pulsing,
a soul waiting to be born from Mother Time.

An ageless face
in ancient stooped body,
the folds in robe gray,
betraying misshapen form,
leaning into the future of creation
while rooted in the present eternity.

She speaks not openly
though wind and breath,
rock and tree know her song
and speak for her at times
to those who have ears to hear.

All do, in their time.

For her voice creates the breath.
Her song none can mistake
if they listen to the breath within their own form.
Its rhythm is magic,
the timing of a life,
perfect in its signature.

All that is required:
an open heart and a raised hand
inviting her entry.

She abides only where asked,
otherwise, shifts at her own pace,
her own wisdom,
smiling at the folly of the forgetful.

THREADS OF TIME

Thin the threads of weave between times,
dimensions of then and now
and forever on.
Our place is merely microsecond in the cosmic wheel
much like a mosquito's time
to our eye.

So thin, yet waste so much of the hour sands
in worry and scheme, running and paying the piper,
forgetting the beat
of our own drum,
the breath and rhyme
of our own heart.
forsaking the minute grain
of time that is our present.

The grave calls
to the next existence
too soon.
Still we scurry not in our own direction
Nor even trod a turtle's pace
Until dawn awakens within-

Then some wake, some heed,
some shift, some flow, and some,
never even catching its glimpse,
slumber still.

THE BLACK SONG

The Black Song
             echoed across Time
the black song heard
             in the depths of mind,
A complex melody
             beating out the ages:
hymns few will perceive
             in the heart
And the Black Song
             echoed across Time.

She heard its darkness
Yet discerned between the beats
Light's rhythm too.
             For black cannot be
             without white,
And she wept
a smile through her tears.
Her heart understood
and the black Song
             echoed across Time.

She, he creator of the
             pattern of the song
Her horn spread
             open to the winds
gathering into tunnels
             all sound
to sift the perfect meaning
             Evolving round and round
             in Timelessness,
and the Black Song
             echoed across Time.

GOLDEN DARKNESS

Golden darkness appeals to me
from my own heart's reverie.
Where it may lead, I do not know.
Yet, to follow, I must go
into worlds as yet unseen
as only few go in between

The veils so thin, from here to there,
Thickly adorned once, now threadbare,
make it time for some to enter,
circling closer to the centre
of all time and space that spin
to find still silence there within,
where abounds creation's mess,
birthed to form in golden darkness.

ONWARD STILL

Onward and beyond,
we come and go.
The borders still enclose
sacred spaces
where none may trod
save owner's sandals;
Nor enter in
by ordinary means
lest judgement's walls
and expectations
fall or melt away
in love and understanding.
One may approach the way.

The path is not so easy
nor difficult to perceive
if one allows a thing to be
as butterflies are free.

The depth of a sanctuary,
its endless light or dark,
The knowing of another's altar
as if walking in one's shoes,
is a rare insight gifted to few.

Love goes way and beyond
if out of human bounds allowed.
the meeting of souls incomprehensible.

Not so,
in rarer realms,
Time and memory,
Birth and Death spaces,
Flight
and the gift of the unsubstantial.

OUR TIME

Rays of a new dawn on our horizon
Day by day, step by step, upon the sand
In timelessness,
    A new rhythm, a wider perspective,
Freedom in being.

    Raven and eagle,
darkness and light,
wombs of birthing anew
    in aloneness,
sharing celestial sun and volcanic depths;
consciousness shared
in a language inadequate
as baby steps in learning to be free
and express truth of selves
so complex and vulnerable.

To live in life's classroom
minute by minute
present to moments of joy,
tears of hurt, rages of madness,
defenses of confusion,
risks of self-disclosure,
is an intense endless revelation:
a course in mystery
and enlightenment.
A lesson in freeing and being freed,
faith and trust tested in fire.

Every moment spoken in truth
has the potential to change
what might have been the next moment
Or what might have been understood in the last.
Light of a new dawning
barely grasped,
yet raising hope and excitement
in possibility.

Time, love's friend,
in the act of unfoldment,
pressures none.
The journey of a thousand miles
begins with one step, the ancients say,
not revealing the magnitude of that step
nor the speed of reaching the next.
A pause or a step back
to reflect,
A wait upon the will of heaven
is not unseemly
for time beholds truth
in its hidden places
and love calls it out.

Joy is truth in freedom
even through tears
or beyond them.
Dawn rises to noon
fully expressed.
Joy dances toward the midnight
Ever seeking
a new day's truth
unfolding.

TO YOU

I hold you within the hands of my heart
uncaged
in a wide circle of light
 that the colours of your mighty sun
may flow freely
through darkness and light,
 Gently enfolded in love
from sunset through sunrise
returning on and on.

My hand reaches always for yours
across chasms
and impassable seas.
Love makes the bridge:
the words from the soul,
the circle of the Tao completes.

We
Cradle the fragile magic
now shadowed,
now glaring,
now softly embracing,
understand its mystique
and its guise.

It turns much like the sun's
intimate cycle with the moon,
ebb and flow like tides
yet touching,
feeling,
knowing,
as cupped hands near embrace.

Love circles round
and remains
as I
ever faithful.

MEMORY

A box, handcrafted,
Empty of time,
Holding nothing
Yet holding everything

A spiralling universe through rings
O a never ending story,
Love in Action.

I do not who you are to me, and I do.
Why we run so along the path together
Separated roots at crossroads,
Meeting again at the edges
Like our meeting at the misty worlds on the shore,
Children at play in sand long ago,
Where elves and trolls were unheard of,
save by ourselves,
(Do they still dwell, do you know?)
lovers at fires of the dream.

Another box, once gifted
Holds now treasures or those days,
early days of our history.
    Imagine that! We have a history.
    We are the stuff of myth
    and a still evolving story.

How many times, do you think,
have we trod, danced, flown together
in timeless realms before the now?

A look into the core of the box reveals:

There is comfort. There is hope.
A circle unbroken,
expanding.

Eye in the centre radiating eternally,
shifting creation
with every tiny gesture of unfoldment.
A crack in the center,
An earthquake fault:
A dimensional gateway
for all who are brave.
Rays of sun shoot forth form that eye
Life giving tree.

Before time was, we were.
You taught me wisdom
long before I came forth,
only to forget that knowing,
and find it again through you.

You are old to me,
an ancient oracle, silent, aloof
until time, urgency,
discernment of right action
calls your word forth,
lessons long honed in your inner worlds.

You are to me, challenge,
A mirror to my self-discovery,
my self-creation.
You let me away with nothing,
accepting.

In your very stance
You induce me to own mine,
to stand.

You see me more
than I see myself.

A kind mirror
Gently unmasks illusion.
Awakening.

How weary you must be
Of my circles of unseeing,
My forays of doubt,
my endless inquiry.
How resistive of my traps,
my wilful ways,
selfish demands,
childish ploys.

And do I not often resist?

All is inside.
As you see—
may I learn to see it
for me.

I am grateful for the reflection.

LET THE MIRROR FALL

Shatter illusion this night.
Another mask has fallen open.
A river of passion flows forth unbridled,
and with it, great perception:
I AM all
as I am myself.

> He who walks with me
> reflects, like a pool, pieces,
> images of myself
> forgotten;
> some wretched,
> some wondrous,
> some holy.
>   It is the dark face
that is difficult to behold;
>   The magical,
hard to believe.
Yet it is me,
an incomparable composition.

A work of art
no other hand could shape
no other eye could vision
but that of the tapestry mistress
of my own soul
in her quiet conferences
with the ways of the will.

> He speaks of art and poetry
> in the same way I witness
> the unfolding of my being.
I have that same passion
for discovery of my language,
my blot on the page.
My failure is over analysis,
left brain critique
of all I am and am not.

Discernment has its place
if one acts upon it
wisely.

I am the single, most important
creation of my life
and worth all the sweat, blood, and tears
that an artist may shed over his masterpieces.
I am not less
for lack of worldly achievements
or creative legacies.

For what I can share
from the abyss of experience
the inner journey of a soul bound to trust itself,
will be truth for some,
a tiny shaft of wisdom's light,
flint for striking a heart's courage,
a hope that Love endures.

> He who walks with me
> trips his own path of soul.
> His words, his art speak
> in a different language and form
> yet is the same journey.

> "In his works,
> Wisdom fuses Love and Power
> into the singular moment of eternity."

> He struggles to birth
> his gift of expressing from
> "behind the eyes"
> the wordless place of imagery;
> an endless kaleidoscope :
> life, death, void, present, past;
The world of the god hunter
and hermitage of the prophet,
> Spirit's child.

To keep it pure,
    to express being
    the wealth of who he is,
beyond the mortal
yet honouring in great love
all that is human.

The mystery of oneness
that soul and hearts cannot deny
that mirrors the eternal,
like crystals revealing many facets
in the light of the same sun.
Shatter one mirror,
One becomes many more,
More colour, more light.
I shift the focus,
Let the mirror fall.

FOLLOW THE WATER

You,
a lone kayaker
skim the edges of reality
in silence
A prayer raised
in Being
One with the craft
one with the water.

You are the depth
and the width,
the spirit's arrow
and its quiver home.

Breathing
your heart's rhythm
in ecstasy
with breath of the Mother,
    her waters
    the womb,
    the steady rock
    ever shape-shifting
    its appearance.

Your depths encompass
    unknown vastness;
where you have wandered before
    forgetfulness and fear
stalked you and hooked your eyes,
Where you sank in the great silent abyss
    and formed your magic
        in secret.
A language unique,
    your soul tongue,
a limitless landscape of your own creation.

You long again that space
where the mind sleeps.
You soar in deeper places
        below the masks,
understanding water's mysteries,
        the treachery and the glory.

Colours of your rainbow seem murky
save in the womb of your heart
        yet sparks fly
                in dusty rivulets
between illusion and the mind's web.
The voices of passionate creation
streak in butterfly wings.

Out of depth
waters flow brighter.
        Death masks Life.
        Dark the mirror for Light.
Carry both
in streamlined twist of fire and ash.
Float them on the calm waters of time
and behold,
You are born.
The cycle of you
ebbs once more
and rises.

LOVE WAITS

Love, like the soul, is mystery.
Love, in its finest eternal quality, dwells therein.
The heart expresses
its many guises:
A burning flame of passion
to the whispering wind of a hand stroke on a cheek,
A sigh of compassion
to a strong stand of support,
Understanding,
seeking only the highest and best.
Love reigns always.
In silence it waits,
enduring
yet ever responsive.
Tossed and torn, given false account often
in the ebb and flow of human tides,
Love endures and seeks ever to flow.

Love is the soul expressing
through the heart, the hands, the voice,
the little things
and the big ones.
Its mystery and its sanctity, boundless,
Its expressions myriad as grains of sands on the beach,
each of them coloured by the temple in which it dwells.
Yet Love is a river connecting everything and everyone
As, to be true to thine own self,
is loving everyone else.
Unhappy is love contained behind mortal's walls.
So tied to soul,
If unfreed,
    Love understands,
        and therefore waits.

KEY

Love is essence
Awareness the key

Beware of ego labels
That separate

We are One
We seek Inside

As above, So below
As within, So without

Tread lightly
As you create
Where you walk

The foot prints left
Come back to you
As others may follow
Where you lead
In their innocence blind

Let your heart lead
The best you can
Intention and action
Spiral in layers
You go whence you came
Eternal being.

RESTORE

Restored,
the faith in wings
as I delve to secure roots.

The wind,
breathed in,
stormed the chaos of illusion,
unearthed
the citadel,
where sat an old wise woman
by a pool
drawing in the dirt.
A circle, a cycle, a plan of flow,
the wheel of the seasons,
the directions of the world.

Bid me create,
unshield my own artistry
along side hers

And behold,
the priestess arose,
the knower of beyond and below.

I am forming,
yet to yield will
to divine craft in unison,

We honour the higher part.

HEART WISDOM

Walk, sing and carry a big stick.
The trees listen and the eyes of the sky watch and hear.
Invisible beings and creatures of earth
lend their gifts of silence, reverence and calm assurance
to one who offers song of seeking and treasuring
                            What is.

        Sit still, breathe and inspire the wind. The sun sets her glory
and the abiding moon puts on her face.
Night walkers emerge from shadows bringing forth
their magic of dew, refreshment and inspiration
to one who offers silence to the heart of the earth
in the web of dark.

STAR MUSING

Singular star the dark, are you, too, depressed in lonely stare?
I think not for you raise hope in many a stargazer,
lost or not, a yearn, a prayer even:
all of which can serve to move a universe,
a heart and at the very least, a stone.

The heart of the tree is what I seek,
its pulsing rhythm unique
yet one with other hearts.
I say I am the tree.
The tree holds me along with my attention.
Awareness of a rock holds me too.
I am rock.
From earth I came. To earth I will return.
But what if I'm a star
        bounded by earth form?

RISE

To rise with the night wolf
and run.
That is desire,
freedom from prying lights.
Alone in the nothingness
of shadows,
I and me, the dreamer,
are one.

To dim even the prison beacon within,
owing to no one,
service or care
but to hunt for my own sake.

To take what night offers
in silence, vastness,
the open orb of moon,
unsheltering passion
and dream.

To attend the vision,
value what day has shunned
in my worm-like existence
where weakness and fear dominate,
strength consumed
in holding back
in deference to secure conformity.

To restore what slow,
is seeping away through disuse and disbelief.
To honour, in rare moment,
the true worth of myself.

THE HOLLOW

Inside the hollow
I gather,
from expanding universe,
vital energies
loving, filling.
I cast out
harming forces
decaying, draining.

Inside the hollow
I dance a fire.
I am the flame,
a glowing form
enduring.

I grow,
flicker,
burst.

I lighten a burden
as wax burns away;
trims the pain.

I float.

Inside the hollow
I sink
sensuously
into the mire
of my forming
washed deliciously
in the flow.

Inside the hollow
I am
life-giving, nurturing,
sensual Woman

surfacing power.

Inside the hollow
I am huge,
a boundless
timeless space,
an overflowing cup.

I am abundance.

Inside the hollow
I am the wind,
the centre of the wind,
the source.

I am the movement,
the poem,
the still.

Inside the hollow
I am free
I am free.

The hollow
I am.

THE WISE ONE SPOKE

Wood hath hope.
Ages forth and back
through the mysteries of time
float the waves divine.

Bow low to earth
my sister wood.
Taste of the evening dew.
Touch the waves
as they lap at your feet.

Float on.
Send thy message upon the wind
to the angels that dwell on high.
Douse all your roots
in the morning light.
Divinity shall be yours.

****

A tree is sacred gift:
Bridges earth to sky,
both God's creation,
dust to cloud.

Its meaning lost to you,
for stillness
you cannot abide
yet a moment,
alone in the solace of silence,
the mystery to enter.

1

Hold the seed in warm, wet palms.
Breathe on it, love.
Shine light upon it
with eyes of wonder.
Plant it in soil nurtured
in the divine gardens of your heart.
Trust it. Believe in its potential.
Water it daily with loving words.
Gently,
persistently draw what it offers,
pruning it as it blooms.
It will start small
but grow into eternity,
yielding greater and greater harvest.
  Use well what it offers
   or it will wither,
   though a seed remains.

2

Do not go to your death, early
Before you have accomplished what is yours to do—
Said what is yours to say,
Your life fully lived.

Listen to the restlessness.
Attend the silences.
Enter both darkness and light.
Do what the inner spirit prompts
  Even uncertain and fearful
for there is life in it for you.

It is sometimes easier to remain
shriveled than to drink fresh,
life-giving waters,
  But it bears no fruit, no joy.
So choose well.

3

Holy, then, is creation,
    sacramental as earthen forms
Without imagination's leap
life is stifling,
rendered rigid by lack of New Vision,
    new forms;
an uninspired merry-go round to nowhere.

    Which pony will be the one to break loose?
      follow inner vision to new scapes?

Praise be for the one who takes the Leap.
    Small changes.
        Small challenges?
          Perhaps
Ripples in the water.
            But, ah, the life stirs.

4

Believe. You of little faith.
We have come for life in abundance.
    Choose life, therefore.
I come to remind you as child of Source,
endowed you are with sacred power.
    Love. Forgive. Create.
Leave your fears
      of death,
      of dark hollows.
Let go of limited visions,
        Ego strings.
See the gifts I have given,
    Live fully.
Let no the mundane bind imagination,
    Or limit your soul's wingspan.
Look, Leap, fly.
There is more . . . than what you were taught,
    More than is mirrored by powers of society.

Few the voices but growing in number
Dare to be ONE . . . it is your birth right.
    Fear not. I AM with you.
    You have ALL you need.

5

In the fertile dark of the abyss is the Sanctuary of Self,
the cauldron of all possibility,
where all potent gifts await our transforming awareness.

Enter the void. Embrace the process.
Be free of illusions and limitations in stillness.
Be aware.
Beyond projections all you are is here now.
All you create is here now. Within!

Be still and know!

THE DANCER

I feel dancing in my soul,
music in whispers
rhythm in my body.

Impossible to tell
the urgency within
waiting to explode:
Fountain of emotions,
carousel of vibrations
tossing, turning,
twirling in a whirlwind
of fantasy
visions, phantoms, echoes
calling, wailing.

Which to follow?

Closing eyes upon the deluge,
soft voice rises:
time to be still.
Dancer in the eye of the storm
is the eye of the storm.

Silence,
the beat between the waves.
Slowly
the heart emits a song,
the sound of which is beauty:
magic of the soul.

The dancer intuits the tune.
Feet create the steps
that journey home.

Through all the dissonance
the dancer lives the dance
known all along.

ALCHEMY

I am crystal
clear
tuned to the wind
    Transforming.
    Transmuting,
        Alchemist.

I am grown in faith,
atop this mountain,
and sliding down again.
        Eternal Beginner.

I am unbound
and unbinding
tightropes of inflexible illusion
      Revisioning the past.
      Gateway home.

I am the within
and the outer form
spirit manifested.
      One with all.
        Being Me.

I am that I am;
there is no other
to be me.
      Earthed stardust.
        Born to shine.

I am. I am. I am.
      Mirror to you.

FLY FREE

Fly high above the fray.
Peer. Perceive all vantage points
in which all ways lead, connecting
to the same source.

Look long into the dark mirror
through which shafts of light
reflect and refract all truth.

Walk the earthen path
in moccasin clad feet
which can feel the heart beat
of the Mother
and know home.

Listen to the whispers
of your heart wind
to hear the music of the spheres,
the lullaby to inner peace.

Follow . . .
Your destiny awaits . . .

Simplicity
Silence
Flow
One.